Connecting
WITH
LONELINESS:
A GUIDED JOURNAL

Connecting

WITH

LONELINESS:

A GUIDED JOURNAL

PROMPTS TO DISCOVER SELF-LOVE,
BUILD CONNECTION, AND EMBRACE JOY

JESSIE EVERTS, PHD, LMFT

Illustrations by Esté Macleod

ROCKRIDGE PRESS

For general information on our other products and services or to obtain technical support, please contact our Customer Care Department within the United States at (866) 744-2665, or outside the United States at (510) 253-0500.

Rockridge Press publishes its books in a variety of electronic and print formats. Some content that appears in print may not be available in electronic books, and vice versa.

TRADEMARKS: Rockridge Press and the Rockridge Press logo are trademarks or registered trademarks of Callisto Media Inc. and/or its affiliatein the United States and other countries, and may not be used without written permission. All other trademarks are the property of their respective owners. Rockridge Press is not associated with any product or vendor mentioned in this book.

Interior and Cover Designer: Regina Stadnik
Art Producer: Samantha Ulban
Editor: Sean Newcott
Production Editor: Mia Moran
Production Manager: Riley Hoffman

Illustrations © 2020 Esté Macleod
Author photo courtesy of Lucy Lao

ISBN: Print 978-1-64876-867-5
R0

For everyone who
feels lonely sometimes.
You are so much more
than that.

CONTENTS

INTRODUCTION VII

PART 1
CONNECTING WITH YOURSELF 1

PART 2
REWRITING YOUR STORY 43

PART 3
EMBRACING YOUR JOY 87

PART 4
CONNECTING WITH CONFIDENCE 127

REFERENCES 169

INTRODUCTION

Welcome! This guided journal is all about building connection, first to yourself, then to others, and then to new opportunities. You might have arrived here because you have been feeling a little lonely. Loneliness is a common experience, and the solution to this feeling is not outside of us, but rather within—your deepest, most meaningful, and most committed relationship is with yourself. At the end of this guided journey, I hope you feel like the best possible version of yourself so you can connect with other people—friends, family, colleagues, romantic partners, peers, neighbors, and strangers—in all of the ways you wish to.

As a marriage and family therapist, I have worked with many people who are struggling with loneliness. Some are physically isolated from family or friends. Some haven't yet had a fulfilling romantic relationship. Some feel alone even when they're surrounded by people. The common theme I see among those experiencing loneliness is an internal sense of disconnection. This journal will help you develop self-awareness, self-love, and self-compassion so that you feel confident, content, and connected.

Journaling is a wonderful practice that provides a space to express and hold your thoughts. We don't always know the ins and outs of what we are thinking, or working through, until we see it written down, and this process allows for deeper reflection. This journal includes a variety of thought-provoking prompts and exercises, inspirational quotes, and positive affirmations to help you connect with yourself on a deep, satisfying level. It is divided into four parts, each building progressively to facilitate meaningful exploration. In addition to guiding you in self-reflection, this journal will help you rewrite your experience from a hopeful point of view, embrace joy and happiness, and open up to new experiences and opportunities with a sense of confidence and curiosity.

I hope you find this journal to be a valuable investment in yourself and your happiness. Recognizing that you want to feel more connected is a great first step and letting go of loneliness to welcome more joy into your life can be a wonderful journey.

PART 1

CONNECTING ==WITH== YOURSELF

Let's begin this journey, together, to help you build connections and embrace more joy and positivity in your life. The first part of this book is about connecting with yourself, because creating better connections with others starts with you. To connect with someone else on a deeper level, you have to first know yourself deeply. This section will give you some prompts and ideas to begin a journey of self-exploration, with the goal of feeling more in tune and secure with yourself.

"Searching all directions with one's awareness, one finds no one dearer than oneself."

—The Udāna

ENVISION CONNECTION

Think about what connection means to you. What would the best kind of connection feel like or look like? How would you know if you felt connected to someone in that way? Write down your thoughts about what connection looks like for you, and then examine your thoughts and identify three goals you'd like to achieve by the time you finish this journal.

GOALS FOR SELF-CONNECTION

Rewrite those same three goals from page 3 again but with yourself as the object of connection. If you wrote, "I want to have someone to talk to," you might instead write, "I want to be able to talk to myself." Consider what it would feel like to be more connected to yourself and, as a result, more connected to others.

_____

_____

_____

_____

_____

_____

"Ultimately, your independence
comes from you knowing who you are
and you being happy with yourself."

—Beyoncé

MEDITATE FOR SELF-CONNECTION

Sit or lie down somewhere quiet where you will be uninterrupted. Close your eyes, or gaze at something in your environment. Inhale deeply and hold it for a moment before releasing it fully. Breathe naturally in a relaxed manner.

Observe your body with patience, with acceptance, and without judgment. If judgmental thoughts arise, notice them, and then gently release them. Observe yourself from a place of calm and compassion, remaining open to whatever you are feeling in this moment.

When you feel ready, place a hand on your heart and give thanks for taking time to connect with yourself.

WHAT GETS IN THE WAY

When you think about being kind to yourself, what obstacles get in the way? What doubts, fears, or concerns make it difficult to experience love for yourself? Say, "I love myself," and see what thoughts or feelings emerge that feel like barriers to that sentiment. Write them down here.

OVERCOME OBSTACLES WITH SELF-COMPASSION

Look at your list of obstacles on page 6. Imagine that a friend told you they were struggling with those same obstacles. What would you tell them to affirm that they are worthy of connection and love? How would you support them? Write down your response to each obstacle as if you were speaking compassionately to a friend. Then say each response to yourself while looking into a mirror.

MAPPING YOURSELF

Write out as many descriptors as you can to best describe yourself in each of these areas:

Work/Education

_____
_____
_____
_____
_____
_____

Free Time/Recreation

_____
_____
_____
_____
_____
_____

Personal Growth/Spirituality

_____
_____
_____
_____
_____
_____

Mental/Physical Health

_____
_____
_____
_____
_____

Relationships

_____
_____
_____
_____
_____

YOUR STRENGTHS ARE MANY

Think of your strengths—as many as you can. These may be things you like about yourself, compliments others have given you, or abilities that make you unique. Reflect on all the positive attributes you can identify about yourself and write them down—without qualifiers or reservations—as strengths you possess.

I am . . .

BUILDING YOUR STRENGTHS ON THE INSIDE

Look back at the list of strengths you created on page 9. Mark any strengths that help you connect with or relate to other people—such as "I am considerate" or "I am loyal"—with a star. Write down those strengths that you starred here as actions toward yourself. Then write an example of how you can use each strength internally. For example, if you are considerate, declare that you will be considerate toward yourself by doing something nice for yourself after a challenging day.

SAVOR YOUR STRENGTH

Engage in an activity that you enjoy and are good at. Whether it is creative, physical, or empathetic, make a plan to enjoy some time pursuing that interest. While you are doing it, take time to appreciate yourself for allowing yourself to enjoy your strength.

STRENGTH-BUILDING EXERCISES

Reflect on what mental, physical, and emotional strength means to you. Consider when you feel strongest in each area. Write down what activities or challenges help you build strength in each one.

Mental Strength:

_____

_____

_____

Physical Strength:

_____

_____

_____

_____

Emotional Strength:

_____

_____

_____

_____

SMALL STRENGTH IS STILL STRENGTH

On days when we feel more self-doubt, loneliness, exhaustion, or stress, tapping into our inner strength might be tough. On such days, our goals might be smaller: to get out of bed, to shower, to call one friend. It takes real strength to do even these small things if your body or mind is telling you not to. Write down all the things you routinely accomplish on such days, no matter how minor. Let each accomplishment be a reminder of how you are showing up for yourself.

USING AFFIRMATIONS

We can sometimes be tough on ourselves without meaning to be. We might have negative thoughts or beat ourselves up when things don't go our way. Write down some of the negative things you've told yourself this week. Then look at each statement and think about whether the thought is even true. Write a positive, uplifting thought with which to replace each negative thought.

I can be my own best friend.

CREATE A SELF-LOVE JAR

Make a container from an unused jar, vase, canister, or fish-bowl. Decorate the container to your liking and place it in a high-visibility spot in your home. Each day, write a positive message to yourself and put it in the jar. It can be an affirmation, a note recognizing something you did well, or a positive feeling or experience you had. When you fill the jar, or when you need a boost, take out the messages and read them to yourself.

COMPLIMENTS TO YOU

Think about compliments or praise you have received and how it felt to receive them. Did you feel proud? Shy? Undeserving? Write down as many compliments as you can remember receiving. Read over them with openness and acceptance. Allow yourself to believe and trust that each one is true.

DO A RAIN MEDITATION

Give yourself five to ten minutes to do the following practice.

Sit or lie down somewhere quiet and comfortable. Close your eyes or gaze at something soothing in your environment. Inhale deeply and hold your breath for a moment before releasing it fully. Allow yourself to breathe naturally and in a relaxed manner. As you move through the meditation, observe the four steps of **RAIN**:

R is for Recognize. Look inward and reflect on what sensations you feel in your body. Recognize the emotions you are experiencing.

A is for Accept. Allow whatever emotions and sensations you recognized to simply be. Acknowledge their presence. Accept what you're feeling as part of you.

I is for Investigate. Notice where in your body you feel the emotions. Look into it with gentle curiosity. Are these feelings familiar? Ask yourself whether they might be trying to let you know something about yourself.

N is for Nurture. What kind of care would feel good to you in this moment? What form would that take? Some kind words or thoughts, reassurance, deep breathing, a hug, or some gentle physical touch might be in order. Take time to offer yourself whatever feels right to you.

"How you love yourself is how you teach others to love you."

—Rupi Kaur
Milk and Honey

Reflect on this quote and write down what it means to you.

ENGAGING IN SELF-CARE

Taking care of ourselves is one way that we show ourselves love. It also allows us to notice how it feels to receive love and what forms of care and kindness feel best. Review the list of self-care activities here and select the ones you like best. Add any that are helpful for you.

- Spending time in nature
- Listening to soothing music
- Taking a long bath or shower
- Exercising
- Enjoying scented candles or oils

- Cooking or baking
- Listening to a guided meditation
- Reading a good book
- Talking with someone you love
- Spending time with a pet

DISCOVER NEW WAYS TO SELF-CARE

Look back at the list of self-care activities on page 19. Mark ones that you don't usually do but would like to try. Make a plan to do one of these new activities today, and when you're done, reflect on how it made you feel.

I am learning how to love myself.

IDENTIFYING BARRIERS TO SELF-CARE

Even if we know we need some time to recharge and relax, we may have difficulty prioritizing ourselves. Reflect on what tends to get in the way of practicing self-care for you. Write down any obstacles to doing at least one self-care activity each day.

BREAKING DOWN INTERNAL BARRIERS

Look at the barriers to self-care you identified on page 21, and see if any are internal barriers or thoughts. Copy them here. If you didn't identify any thought barriers, reflect and write down any thoughts that keep you from practicing self-care. Then write an affirmation or positive message to counteract each thought.

PRACTICING COMPASSION WHEN YOU FEEL UNWORTHY

Do you sometimes doubt if you deserve care and compassion? Self-doubt commonly arises under stress. What would you say to a close friend who told you they felt unworthy of love? Write down how you would respond to this friend and give that same compassion to yourself.

YOUR BEST SELF

Imagine that in this exact moment you are your best self. Think about how you would like to act, feel, or respond to others. Write down these aspirations. Do some of these descriptors already apply to you? What would make you feel closer to your best self? Resolve to act as if you are already your ideal self to see how that feels. Reflect on what parts of the shift are internal and how you can make this adjustment.

CHANGING YOUR THOUGHTS TO CHANGE YOUR FEELINGS

Write down any harsh or negative thoughts you may have noticed lately. How did they make you feel? For each thought you come up with, consider how shifting your internal dialogue, even just slightly, might change how you feel. Sometimes all it takes is changing one negative word to a positive one, giving yourself a little more credit, or reflecting through a more caring perspective. Write down the shifted thoughts and reflect on how these versions make you feel.

YOGA POSES FOR SELF-LOVE

If it feels comfortable for you, try the child's pose (*Balasana*) to feel grounded and reflective. Take a tabletop position by getting on your hands and knees, then sit back on your heels, straightening your arms out in front of you. You can move your knees apart as wide as you'd like. Place your forehead on the floor or on your crossed arms. Allow yourself to rest here, cultivating a feeling of care and kindness toward yourself and toward your inner child.

If this pose is not comfortable for you, you can sit cross-legged with one hand on your heart to rest and reflect.

YOUR SELF-LOVE LANGUAGE

Reflect on how you feel most cared for. Is it through kind words, physical affection, thoughtful gifts, time spent together, or helpful acts? Identify ways you can show yourself love according to your preferred love language and write them down. When you engage in these activities, remind yourself that this is an expression of self-love, and contemplate how it makes you feel to receive this love from yourself.

PRACTICING GRATITUDE

Write about three people, objects/possessions, or circumstances for which you are grateful. Jot down why you are grateful for each and what other emotions or sensations come to you when you feel this gratitude. Then extend this practice to yourself by writing one thing that you are grateful for about yourself. Why are you grateful for this part of you, and what does this gratitude feel like?

CONSIDERING YOURSELF

Consider the following questions and write down your reflections:

How do you feel when someone compliments you?

How do you deal with criticism?

When do you feel most comfortable being yourself?

How do you feel when you make a mistake? What do you do?

What is an accomplishment that you feel proud of? Why?

Reflect on your answers and see if you learn anything new about yourself.

ACCEPTING YOUR CHALLENGES

We all have parts of ourselves that can be more challenging to celebrate. You might think of these unique aspects of yourself as weaknesses, flaws, or limitations. Write about aspects of yourself that you view in this way, but practice acceptance and compassion toward these parts of yourself. Write some thoughts about your challenges through this accepting, compassionate lens.

I am a beautiful work in progress.

FEELING ACCEPTANCE

Think about someone who accepts you fully. How do you know that they accept you? What do they say or do to show you that? How do you feel when you are around them? If no one from your present comes to mind, think about someone from the past. Write about what it feels like to be fully accepted and loved, just as you are.

FIND YOUR PEACEFUL PLACE

Take a few moments to get comfortable and participate fully in this visualization. Think about a place where you feel most at peace. Visualize yourself in that setting, allowing yourself the feeling of peace that you have when you're actually there.

Bring to mind as many details as possible about this peaceful place. Notice your breathing and the sensations in your body that make you feel at peace. Reflect on what is calm and comforting about this place. The experience of peace you feel when you are there is something you can bring with you anywhere you go.

NOTES ON PEACE

Think back to visiting your Peaceful Place. Describe the place that is most peaceful to you, in all its details and sensations. Next, describe the feelings you experienced when visualizing yourself there. Write as much as you can about the feelings, so that you can recreate the experience of being there.

"The truth is: Belonging starts with self-acceptance. Your level of belonging, in fact, can never be greater than your level of self-acceptance, because believing that you're enough is what gives you the courage to be authentic, vulnerable, and imperfect."

—Brené Brown
Daring Greatly

PRACTICING SELF-VALIDATION

An important aspect of connecting with yourself is validating your feelings—letting yourself know that there is a reason for what you're feeling and that you have a right to feel that way. Write down some feelings you have noticed in yourself recently. Then jot down the reasons behind those feelings—whatever led you to feel that way. Finally, write down a validating statement about each emotion, such as "My emotions are valid because . . ." or "I have a right to feel this way because . . ."

YOUR WORD COLLAGE

Make a word collage using all the ideas that come to mind about yourself when you feel accepted. Finish this sentence with as many words as you can: "When I feel accepted and loved, I am . . ."

PRACTICING RADICAL ACCEPTANCE

It can sometimes be difficult to allow our feelings to just be, or to embrace our challenges. In times when we feel more sensitive, we should practice radical acceptance, a completely open and accepting view of ourselves, without question or reservation. Write down some examples of when you might need to practice this kind of self-acceptance and how you can do it.

I accept myself as I am.

CONDUCTING A SELF-CHECKUP

Take a moment to check in with yourself about the goals for self-connection you set at the beginning of this journal. How are you progressing toward those goals of connecting with yourself? If you have done well, give yourself some recognition and appreciation. If you have more work to do, write down some measurable, achievable things you can do to reach your goals, and celebrate that you are an incredible work in progress.

STACK THE DECK

Write some of the positive affirmations that have been most helpful for you on notecards. Decorate the notecards however you'd like. Post them around your living space so that you will come across them when you need them—or when you least expect to, so that you will surprise yourself with positive messages.

THE POWER OF OUR SHARED HUMANITY

Kristin Neff is a researcher who studies self-compassion and notes that it has three parts: "mindfulness," "self-kindness," and "common humanity." This third part connects us to others through a compassionate lens. Bring to mind the idea that there are many others out there who might be feeling and even struggling in similar ways to you. Write about what this connection to others feels like from a place of self-compassion.

A LOVE LETTER TO YOURSELF

Using the reflections from the first part of this journal, write a love letter to yourself. Discuss the strengths you identified on page 9, any of the things you wrote for your self-love jar on page 15, or growth you have experienced while working through the exercises. Write about each positive aspect of yourself and why you cherish it. How have these gifts benefited you in life? Then write about the ways you will honor your gifts. Use a tone that conveys love and compassion toward yourself.

PART 2

REWRITING YOUR STORY

Y ou have done some great work connecting to yourself in this journal. Now, let's turn toward your future view of yourself and how to make positive, desired changes to both your thinking and your life. In this part, we'll talk about how to rewrite your narrative by challenging and reframing some of the beliefs and fears that might be holding you back from connecting fully to yourself and to others. As you get to know yourself better, you'll continue to write your story each day. It's time to create a story that you love.

"She stood in the storm, and
when the wind did not blow
her way—and it surely has not—
she adjusted her sails."

—Elizabeth Edwards
Resilience

BELIEFS IN YOU

Reflect on beliefs you have about yourself—things you believe to be true, like "I believe I am a good friend," "I believe I'm a failure," or "I believe I'm destined for greatness." Think about things others have said to you that you may have internalized, as well as things you tell yourself about who you are and what you can or can't do. Write as many beliefs about yourself as you can identify. Don't judge the beliefs as you write them, just acknowledge them.

BELIEF SORTING

Thinking about your list of beliefs on page 45, identify those you want to strengthen. If there are some you would like to challenge, write them here. Identify what you would like to change or substitute.

YOUR ELEVATOR SPEECH

How might you describe yourself when you've just met someone? What important things would you want to mention about your life experience? Write something you might say in two to three minutes, or the length of an elevator ride.

THE PARTS OF YOU

Answer the following questions about your life, marking the ones that feel like an important and formative part of who you are:

What is your birth date?

_____

_____

Where were you born?

_____

_____

Who were your first caregivers?

_____

_____

What was your early life like?

_____

_____

What did you like to do in your free time as a child?

_____

_____

Who were your friends/peers as a teenager?

_____

_____

What was your school experience like?

_____

_____

Do you have religious/spiritual beliefs? What are they? Where do they come from?

_____

_____

What have your relationships been like (romantic and/or platonic)?

_____

_____

What do you do for work?

_____

_____

What do you do in your free time? When did you start these hobbies?

_____

_____

BUMPS IN THE ROAD

Reflect on some challenges you have faced in your life that you've overcome. Write about the qualities you possess, or have worked to develop, that have helped you through those bumps in the road. What do they reveal to you about yourself?

REFINE YOUR ELEVATOR SPEECH

Think back to the elevator speech you wrote about yourself on page 47. Are there any changes you'd like to make to it? Add any of the details that feel important from your life experience or challenges you've faced and practice giving this elevator speech to yourself in the mirror. Make eye contact with yourself and think about how you'd like to be received when you first meet someone. Reward yourself with a smile or a reply, such as "It's wonderful to meet you!"

I am unique and interesting.
My story is mine alone.

THOUGHT TROUBLE: SHOULDING

Shoulding is hanging on to beliefs about what you should or shouldn't do, or what others should or shouldn't do. This judgmental thinking builds resentment, guilt, and shame, which keep you from moving forward. Reflect on whether you have fallen into the habit of shoulding yourself, and if so, write down an example.

_____

_____

_____

_____

_____

Solution: Identify what judgment you are making that tells you there is something you should do. Consider whether the judgment is a fact, or if there is a more flexible, nonjudgmental belief you can substitute for it. Write down the alternative belief here and repeat it to yourself when you find yourself preoccupied with shoulds.

_____

_____

_____

_____

_____

AVOID BEING JUDGE AND JURY

Judgments are isolating and damaging to our self-esteem. Judgmental appraisals can cause us to disconnect from others and go into our own thinking or reactions, rather than allowing for connection and understanding. As you go through your day, identify any judgmental thoughts—about yourself or others—that come into your mind, and write them down.

UNLEARNING JUDGMENTS

Think about some of the things you think are good or bad, and right or wrong. Consider what judgments you hold about yourself, your life, and your worth. Write them down. Where do these judgments come from? Are they helpful to you? Think about what feeling each judgment conjures up. Ask whether you would feel differently—more motivated or less down on yourself—if you could drop the judgment altogether.

REPLACING JUDGMENT WITH CURIOSITY

The antidote to judgmental thinking is curiosity. When a self-judgment arises, notice it. Allow it to be and acknowledge that it is there. Then, remembering the RAIN meditation on page 17, ask yourself whether there is some care or nurturing that you need. Accepting your judgmental thoughts is powerful because it allows you to choose whether or not to respond from a place of judgment. How might this practice be helpful in your life?

"You alone are enough. You have nothing to prove to anyone."

—Maya Angelou

Reflect on this quote and write about your thoughts.

_____

_____

_____

_____

_____

_____

_____

_____

_____

_____

_____

_____

_____

_____

THINKING KINDER THOUGHTS

When you have recognized a judgmental thought about yourself, think about whether there might be an alternative, less judgmental substitute. For example, you might replace "Why did I do that?" with a gentler question like "I wonder what motivated me to do that?" Write down some ways you can reframe your judgmental thoughts.

THOUGHT TROUBLE: AVOID CATASTROPHIZING

Catastrophizing is thinking that the worst possible outcome is likely to happen and dwelling on how awful it will be. Ask yourself whether you have catastrophized and provide an example.

_____

_____

_____

_____

Solution: Identify a catastrophic outcome you have been dwelling on, and consider how likely that outcome actually is. If it feels helpful, do some research if there is a credible statistic that identifies how likely this outcome is. Rate the likelihood on a scale from 0 to 100. Then identify what outcomes are more likely to happen. Practice switching from catastrophic beliefs to more realistic thoughts and feeling comforted by the reality that there is often nothing to fear.

_____

_____

_____

_____

FEEL THE PRESENT MOMENT

When you find yourself feeling anxious or having negative thoughts, take time to ground yourself in the present moment. Take in your environment using your five senses. If your mind wanders, gently bring it back to the present moment.

ACKNOWLEDGING YOUR FEARS

List some of your fears. They might be events or experiences that you dread or that cause you distress. They might be concerning thoughts or feelings. They might be full-blown phobias or moments of alarm or fright. After you have written them down, give yourself some care and compassion for acknowledging your fears.

UNDERSTANDING THE EFFECTS OF YOUR FEARS

Consider how your fears motivate you. Do you do anything differently because you have these fears? For each fear you recognized, write about how it affects your life. Give each fear a rating between 1 and 10 based on its effect on your life, 1 being "It doesn't affect my life at all" and 10 being "This fear affects my life all the time."

FLIPPING THE FEAR

Think about being in a situation in which you would need to face one of your smaller fears. While you are imagining a feeling, bring into the scene something that you love or are excited about: a loved one, a special treat, or something happily unexpected, like a puppy or some lovely music. Allow your feeling to shift to a more positive sensation. Write about what might be a welcome surprise if you were in the midst of some discomfort, and how it would make you feel.

"You gain strength, courage, and confidence by every experience in which you really stop to look fear in the face."

—Eleanor Roosevelt
You Learn by Living

FACE THE FEAR

Choose a fear that prompts a feeling of loneliness and that affects your life a small to medium amount. Think about what accommodations you have made for this fear, and plan a way to undo this fear conditioning. If, for example, you usually take the stairs because you're afraid to be in the elevator with other people, make a plan to ride in an elevator just one floor. Carry out your plan, then write about how it went and reward yourself for having faced your fear.

LOWERING YOUR FEAR RATING

Consider if you are accommodating your fears in ways that might not be helpful. If there is a fear that you rated as affecting your life to a higher degree than you would like, how could you lower that rating? As you reflect on what you might do differently, identify what feelings arise. Write about the emotions you feel when you think about making this change.

I am brave. I can have fear and not let it stop me.

CULTIVATE A CONFIDENT AND CAPABLE YOU

When you feel anxious or recognize that you are facing a fear-inducing situation, take a break for a purposeful practice that welcomes the feeling of hope. First, bring to mind how you hope the situation will turn out. Activate your rational brain to counteract the emotions brought up by fear. Next, call to mind an image of yourself as a confident person who can handle this situation. Feel your own power and capability. Write down any words or images that help you recapture this version of yourself.

THOUGHT TROUBLE: BLACK-AND-WHITE THINKING

Another common cognitive distortion is black-and-white thinking. This refers to seeing yourself as having only two options in a situation or seeing only two extreme ways that something can turn out, rather than perceiving the gray area in between that might open up other possibilities. Write down a time you fell into this kind of thinking and how it made you feel.

_____

_____

_____

_____

_____

_____

Solution: Challenge yourself to see the shades of gray in between the two extreme options. Ask someone you trust if they can identify any other choices that you can't.

_____

_____

_____

_____

SEEING SHADES OF GRAY

If there is a situation in your life where you feel caught between two extremes or feel there are only two options, practice looking for the gray area in between. Try combining pieces of each option into different arrangements. What factors make the situation more complex than can be captured by a black-and-white perspective? Write about as many different choices or possibilities as you can.

THE FUTURE YOU

Who do you want to be in the future? Write who you hope to be one year from now. How do you want to feel about yourself? Do you want to envision yourself feeling less alone or more fulfilled? What beliefs or judgments might you need to let go of to become this future you?

ACT AS IF

Take one or two elements from your Future You hopes and goals on page 69, and try acting as if that dream version of yourself is true right now. For instance, if you hoped to feel accomplished in your work, practice feeling as if you have achieved it already. Do something today that Future You might do, and allow yourself to enjoy the feelings of success that you will ultimately feel when you have realized your dream.

PRACTICING GOAL-GETTING

Do you sometimes set goals for yourself that feel too big or too vague? This can get in the way of being or feeling successful—it might not be that you are failing, but that you're not defining success specifically or achievably enough. Think about how you can set a goal that is Specific, Measurable, Attainable, Relevant, and Time-based (or SMART). Be ambitious and realistic!

THOUGHT TROUBLE: JUMPING TO CONCLUSIONS

Another kind of unhelpful thinking is jumping to conclusions, such as assuming that you know what another person is thinking or what will happen in a situation before the facts are in. Reflect on whether you have done this, and give an example of a time when you jumped to a conclusion.

_____

_____

_____

_____

_____

Solution: Examining the facts, rather than making conclusions based on feelings of _what ifs_, can help you see the reality of the situation. Reflect here on the facts that might have led you to act or feel differently in a situation where you jumped to a conclusion. How can you lean into being soothed by the facts?

_____

_____

_____

_____

_____

MORE ON GOAL-GETTING

We sometimes forget to think about what obstacles might come up as we work to reach our goals and what we will do if and when they arise. If we haven't thought ahead, we might give up as soon as things get hard. Looking at the goal you set on page 71, think about what obstacles might arise on your path. Make a plan for how you will deal with these obstacles. Consider how good it will feel to achieve your goal, despite any hurdles you may face.

I can overcome obstacles and achieve my dreams.

TALES FROM THE FIRE

Rewriting your story doesn't mean trying to erase things that happened in the past that were difficult or that created painful memories. In fact, they are part of what make you unique. Think about some of the challenges you have faced in your life and whether there were lessons you learned from those experiences. Write about the good things that have come from hardships in your life.

TELL YOUR STORY IN STONES AND FLOWERS

Gather some materials from your environment: stones or rocks of different shapes and sizes, flowers, leaves, or other decorative items. You can also use pictures or draw these materials if they aren't available. Think about your life story, starting as early as you can. Mark noteworthy but challenging events with stones, and beautiful events with flowers or other decorative items. Choose larger stones or flowers for bigger events, and smaller ones for less significant memories. Go through as much of your life story as you can using these symbols.

Take a picture when you are done. Appreciate the beauty of your life. Your story is a work of art.

FOSTERING SELF-LEADERSHIP

Look at the list of qualities that follows: confidence, calmness, creativity, clarity, curiosity, courage, compassion, and connectedness. These are the eight Cs of self-leadership. You have all of these qualities within you, and when you feel closest to your best self, you likely see them emerge. Identify one or two that you'd like to work on. Think about how you can practice building this trait and write down some ideas or things to try.

REMOVING WALLS AROUND THE SELF

Shame, fear, and pain can keep us from fully connecting to our truest, best selves. Think about whether any of these are barriers to you connecting to your deepest self, and why. Write what feels important about any of these feelings. Recognize that fighting these feelings or covering them up is what gives them power over your life. The best antidote is to accept them as they are, as a part of you. How can you nurture yourself when these feelings arise, rather than putting so much of your energy toward shutting them out or covering them up?

"Fear keeps us focused on the past or worried about the future. If we can acknowledge our fear, we can realize that right now we are okay. Right now, today, we are still alive, and our bodies are working marvelously. Our eyes can still see the beautiful sky. Our ears can still hear the voices of our loved ones."

—Thich Nhat Hanh
Fear: Essential Wisdom for Getting Through the Storm

Reflect on this quote and write about your thoughts.

_____

_____

_____

_____

_____

TAKE A MINDFUL WALK

Take a walk outside. While you walk, be mindful of the things around you. Allow yourself to really see the beautiful sky. Hear all of the sounds. Feel the textures of nature. Take a deep breath and notice how the air feels in your nose and mouth. Recognize that when you are fully mindful of the moment and your environment, it is impossible to ruminate about the past or worry about the future.

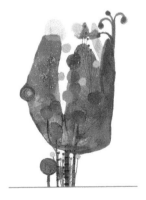

FROM SHAME TO BRAVE

Professor, author, and podcast host Brené Brown has interviewed hundreds of individuals about their feelings of imperfection and shame. She has found that while we all struggle with these feelings, we can develop shame resilience by thinking more critically about why we feel shame and challenging ourselves to bravely move through such feelings. Answer these questions about an area or experience that you feel shame around:

How realistic are my expectations of myself?

_____

_____

_____

_____

Can I be all these things all the time?

_____

_____

_____

_____

Am I describing who I want to be or what others want me to do?

_____

_____

_____

_____

PRACTICING BRAVERY

Write about a situation in which you felt brave. Describe what happened, why you felt brave, and what exactly that bravery felt like to you. What parts of your body come alive when you feel brave? What sensations do you feel? How do you know when you are feeling brave? Bring the feeling to mind and hold it. Recognize that this is the feeling you have when you face and overcome your fears, shame, or other barriers.

CHANGING THE NARRATIVE

Think about a part of your life story that you don't generally share with others, perhaps because it brings up painful feelings of loneliness or isolation. See if certain words strike you as judgmental or negative, and ask whether you can replace them with more helpful alternatives. Read through this part of your narrative as if it were someone else's story, and reflect on how you would want to support or care for them.

I am the author of my own story, and I can bring out the beauty in it.

CONNECT THROUGH STORY

Think about a formative life experience you've gone through and find a written account—a book or blog post—by someone else about a situation that mirrors yours. Reflect on what was similar, what was different, and whether there was something helpful about reading someone else's experience. Did you feel connected to this person as you read? Why or why not?

CHANGING THE OUTLOOK

When you think about making connections with others, what are some thoughts that get in the way? Do you think you are too much or too emotional? Do you feel self-conscious? Write down the thoughts that come into your mind when you think about social situations, and inspect these thoughts for judgments. Write an affirmation that counters each negative thought you identified. Say the affirmation aloud to yourself and believe in its truth.

REWRITING YOUR STORY

Look back at the picture you took of the visual telling of your life story with stones and flowers on page 75. Write your life story, using nonjudgment, acceptance, compassion, and bravery. Take breaks to practice mindfulness and self-care as needed. Allow yourself to make new meaning out of the challenges and difficulties you have faced. Allow your new story to reflect the hope you want to feel as you move forward.

PART 3

EMBRACING YOUR JOY

I hope that you're feeling closer to yourself than you have before. And I hope you are beginning to appreciate all the lovable and unique things about yourself. Keeping in mind your self-exploration and your story, this section will help you find peace and joy within yourself. These skills and feelings will ultimately be with you wherever you go. Being alone does not mean that you have to feel lonely. You are great company!

"Acknowledging the good that you already have in your life is the foundation for all abundance."

—Eckhart Tolle
A New Earth

PINPOINTING YOUR JOY

Think back on your day today and write about a moment in which you felt happiest. What happened that contributed to your feeling of joy? What did it feel like in your body? Where were you, and what things did you notice with your five senses at the time? Did you have an impulse to do anything when you were feeling joyful—jump up and down, tell a friend, laugh, or cry? Did you allow yourself to do that?

EXCITING YOURSELF

Reflect on what you are passionate about. What kinds of things excite you, motivate you, and interest you? Choose something in each of those three categories, and write about how you can make time to feed those passions regularly.

USING PEACEFUL IMAGES

Look at some images that you find peaceful—whether they're in an art book, from an internet search, or photographs from your past—and take note of what you are drawn to. What kinds of pictures make you feel at peace? Write about what you like to see to feel calm, and think about how you can make these images more prominent in your life, maybe by saving them to your screens or framing and hanging them around your home.

CREATE A CALM SPOT

Create a calm, peaceful place in your home. It can be as small as a corner with a chair or pillow, or larger, like an entire room, if you have the space. Bring in colors and textures that soothe you, like a soft blue blanket or a peaceful picture of mountains. Aim to create a serene place for all your senses. Spend time in this spot when you are feeling calm or need to find your peace.

MAKING TIME FOR GRATITUDE

Research has shown that practicing gratitude can boost our mental health long-term. Write a list of five things or people for which you are grateful. Add a few notes for each about why you are grateful for this thing or person today. Take a few moments to reflect on your feelings of gratitude for each thing or person on your list, and savor the waves of joy that wash over you.

I am joyful and grateful.

PRACTICING INSIDE-OUT GRATITUDE

Write down five qualities about yourself for which you are grateful. Reflect on why you are grateful for these parts of yourself and how you see them showing up for you when you need them.

GIVE YOURSELF A MINI-CELEBRATION

Look ahead at your week and identify something that you hope to accomplish. Think about how you can celebrate this achievement when you reach it. You might indulge in a small treat, go outside for a nature break, or throw yourself an energizing dance party. Plan your celebration and carry it out when the time comes—you deserve it!

THE ROUTES TO JOY

Holistic psychiatrist Henry Emmons writes in his book *The Chemistry of Joy* about three routes to joy: awareness, compassion, and generosity. Think about how you have practiced these three qualities lately, and ask if you could benefit from paying more attention to one in particular. Make a plan to incorporate this element into your day today and see what a difference it makes.

FOSTERING AWARENESS

Write about ways you can bring your awareness to the feeling of joy in your life. How can you become better at recognizing joy and savoring it or extending it when you do feel joyful? What things bring you joy? How can you give those things more attention or bring them to the forefront more often?

"I celebrate myself, and sing myself."

—Walt Whitman
"Song of Myself"

THE JOY LIST

Make a word collage of the different things that bring you joy. List objects, events, hobbies, foods, possessions, settings, locations, comforts, pets, people, colors, and memories that make you happy. When you get stuck, think through your five senses to see if you might have left out any smells, sounds, sights, tastes, or textures that fill you with positive feelings.

FINDING HAPPY PLACES

With your joy list in mind, look around your space and see whether there are ways to make it more happiness-inducing. Take stock of the items you see and use every day, and determine if they give you a feeling of joy and how you might amplify that feeling. Perhaps you can print and frame a favorite image or quote, or display a beloved item in a more central place in your home.

GIVE YOURSELF A SOUNDTRACK BOOST

Think back through the years to songs that have made you feel happy at different points in your life. With those songs in mind, create a playlist to boost your mood. Include music that makes you feel energized and positive and puts a smile on your face.

PRACTICING OPTIMISM

Write down some pessimistic thoughts you've had this week, and see how you can make them more specific or small-scale. If you wrote, "I'm never going to make any new friends," reframe that statement into one that's more defined, such as, "I don't have as many friends as I'd like right now." This gives you something to work toward. Next write down some positive thoughts you've had this week, and see if you can make them more general. If you wrote, "Sometimes I can be funny," turn that into, "I have a great sense of humor." Finding limits for pessimistic thoughts makes them improvable. And removing limits from positive thoughts makes you more optimistic!

TUNING IN TO OPTIMISM

Pessimism can lead us to focus on the parts of a situation out of our control, instead of the parts we can control. Write about a situation in which you might have felt pessimistic, or like you had little control, and brainstorm what things were within your control in that situation.

FEELING ACCOMPLISHED

Take a few minutes to think about something you're proud of accomplishing over the past year. This can be anything: taking on a new project or role at work, how you handled a conflict, or trying a new hobby. Write about what happened, focusing on your role in it and taking credit for your accomplishments and the feeling of pride they give you.

FINDING THE LITTLE HAPPIES

What are three things that you do daily to make yourself happy? Think through your usual routine and note the parts that you enjoy. Maybe it's drinking a cup of coffee or tea, preparing food, or listening to music. Note as many of these small moments of happiness as you can, and then work to ensure you can do at least three of them each day.

HAVE A BEAUTIFUL DAY

Set aside a day to treat yourself to your favorite, most happiness-producing activities. Make a plan to indulge in as many pleasurable activities as you can. Include self-care, mindfulness, savoring positive feelings, and using all of your senses. Plan your day by the hour, including what you will eat, how you will care for yourself, and which fun activities and hobbies you will enjoy. When the day comes, don't allow outside busyness to interrupt your plan and enjoy the beautiful day you planned.

REFLECTIONS OF BEAUTY

Have you enjoyed your beautiful day of happiness-producing activities yet? (If you haven't, can you set aside time for it this week?) If you have, what did you enjoy most? Did anything get in the way of your happiness or come up unexpectedly? How did you handle that? Were you able to fully enjoy the activities you planned for yourself? Are there elements of your beautiful day that you want to incorporate more into your everyday life?

My life is filled with moments of joy and beauty.

NURTURING YOUR JOY

Consider the things you have identified that make you feel happy. Reflect on them as a part of you that you nurture and care for. Paying time and attention to these things is building your ability to be compassionate and caring. Write some words of affirmation about how practicing self-care and cultivating your happiness is a strength that you are building.

"To love oneself is the beginning
of a lifelong romance."

—Oscar Wilde
An Ideal Husband

ANIMAL ASPIRATIONS

Think about an animal that you admire and find inspiring. What is it about this animal that you admire? What qualities do they have that you wish to embody? Are there any ways in which you are already like this animal? Think about what feelings this animal inspires within you and how their image can encourage you when you need a lift.

COMPLIMENTS TO YOU

Look in the mirror and pay attention to the things that you like about yourself. Compliment yourself on these things out loud. Strive to give yourself one compliment each day when you're getting ready to set a confident and self-affirming tone for the day.

YOUR SLEEPING, EATING, AND MOVEMENT HABITS

Consider your current sleeping, eating, and movement habits. This is not about judging yourself or trying to adhere to a strict regimen. It is about showing yourself care and compassion in daily living. Consider which parts of your sleep, nutrition, and movement are within your control and what achievable changes you might be able to make. Notice how your mood is impacted when you make these changes.

STROLLING DOWN MEMORY LANE

Reflect on one of your happiest memories. Write about what you remember. What made you happy in that moment? What sensations do you recall? What did your happiness feel like? Sit with your memory and savor the feelings of joy that come with it.

_Happiness is a gift I can give to myself
today, tomorrow, and every day._

REVISITING MEMORY LANE

Think back over several of your memories that bring you feelings of joy, and write notes about what made you feel joyful. See if you can identify any themes. Are there certain times, events, people, or activities that tend to be part of your happiest memories? See what patterns or connections you can identify in your past happiness, and write about how you might use those connections to create more opportunities for joy.

DO A MORNING MOTIVATION

Spend five minutes in the morning setting an achievable goal or intention for yourself. If there is a challenge you need to face during the day, think about your plan for tackling it, as well as what obstacles might come up and how you will handle them. If there is not a specific challenge in your day, set an intention or create an affirmation to keep in your mind. Write about your plan in as much detail as you can, and review it at the end of the day to see how it went.

EVENING REVIEW

We often ruminate at night about things that happened during the day—what we wish we would have said or done. It might even keep us from getting to sleep. But we can't turn back time; the best we can do is learn from the past and continue moving forward. When you find yourself ruminating, ask yourself these three questions:

What *did* I do well in the situation?

_____

_____

_____

_____

What could have gone better?

_____

_____

_____

_____

What do I want to try differently next time I'm in that situation?

_____

_____

_____

_____

SELF-COMPASSION BREAK

If you're feeling lonely or have conflict in your relationships, you might internalize a message that you are unworthy of love. This is untrue and cruel. No matter your circumstance, your history, your flaws and challenges, you are deserving of love. Write down any lingering thoughts of unworthiness that you can identify, and then write an affirmation that you can practice to challenge each one.

MAKE AFFIRMATION ART

Make a collage or piece of art out of affirmations that are helpful to you. You can look up affirmations in books or on the internet. Print and decorate quotes or aspirational images, or create the affirmations from scratch, tapping in to your artistic side. Put your collage up somewhere you can view it often to feel inspired.

BUFFERING NEGATIVE FEELINGS WITH SELF-CARE

Identify when you are most likely to experience negative thoughts or feelings during the day. Is it when you are stressed about a task? When you have to interact with someone who is difficult to handle? When you have identified your negativity touch points, think about what precedes these stressful times, and plan for a positive moment of self-care during that preparation phase. Write about what you will do and when you will do it to face stress without taking it on.

ACTS OF SERVICE

What have you done for others that made you feel good? What have others done for you that felt heartwarming? Write down as many acts of kindness and generosity as you can. Think about which acts might be things you can do for yourself.

ENGAGE IN SELF-SERVICE

Make a plan to carry out an act of generosity for yourself. It might be something from the Acts of Service list you made on page 118. It could be something small, like buying yourself flowers to brighten up your room or writing yourself a card with a compassionate message. Carry out your plan and reflect on how it feels to be generous toward yourself, cultivating feelings of deservingness and joy.

FINDING YOUR JOY TIME

Think about when in the day you are most positive, creative, or confident. When do you have the most energy and feel most engaged? It might be tied to a certain time of the day or to performing a certain task. Write about what in the day makes you feel this way and how the positive emotion feels when you are in it.

DO YOU VALIDATE?

Validation, or confirmation that our feelings are justified and okay, can be tough to come by from external sources. Think about what feelings you search for validation of, and what you hope to hear that would make you feel validated. You might just need a "That's okay" or "You have a reason to feel that way." Write down some validating statements that you can say to yourself when you need support or approval.

UNLONELY YOURSELF

When you're feeling low or lonely, reflect on what would feel good to you in that moment. Consider what needs you are demonstrating, whether for physical affection, sharing of ideas, or validation and compassion. Brainstorm how you might be able to meet these needs for yourself—perhaps by giving yourself a hug or neck massage, journaling, or saying affirmations aloud.

GO ON A SOLO DATE

Take yourself out on a solo date to enjoy your own company. It's okay to start small. You might go to the library, a coffee shop, or your favorite restaurant for lunch. Plan a few activities that you enjoy doing by yourself. Let go of any worries or judgments that might come up. Allow yourself to savor this time and reflect on how you feel when you create fun opportunities for yourself.

I am an interesting and remarkable person.

I enjoy my own company.

"Knowing how to be solitary is central to the art of loving."

—bell hooks

All About Love: New Visions

THE ART OF SOLITUDE

There is a difference between enjoying solitude and feeling lonely. Write about the differences you see between solitude and loneliness. What do the two words mean to you? How are they different? Write about feelings you might have when you're in a state of solitude versus in a state of loneliness. What are some situations you might associate with each? Reflect on your answers to see what your important distinctions are between being alone and feeling lonely.

WITH HIGHEST RECOMMENDATION

Imagine that you are being nominated for a prestigious award. Write your own nomination in the third person from the perspective of someone who loves you very much. Write with a compassionate, validating voice that wants the best of you to shine through. Start with these prompts and add in other things that are special and unique about you.

_____ is a _____ individual.
[your name]

_____ has faced many challenges, including:
[your name]

_____

Because of the things they have been through, _____ has learned:
[your name]

_____

_____ has these strengths and unique qualities:
[your name]

_____

In their alone time, _____ enjoys:
[your name]

_____

The world is a better place with _____ in it because:
[your name]

_____

More wonderful things about _____:
[your name]

_____

PART 4

CONNECTING
WITH CONFIDENCE

Now that you have become a good friend to yourself, it's time to take that energy out into the world. The effort you've put into building your self-esteem, self-care, and self-confidence will help you approach others with curiosity and compassion. We'll take this step easy and slow, with lots of reflection and care. But trust that you have the strength and openness to make meaningful connections and take on new experiences. You are an interesting and unique person, and it's time to let that light shine a little brighter.

"Nothing can dim the light which shines from within."

—Maya Angelou

KEEPING YOUR EYE
ON THE PRIZE

Reflect back on the three connection goals you wrote down on page 3. Now that you've gained a greater sense of self-knowledge, does it feel like the goals you made for yourself need to change? Rewrite those goals to better reflect what kind of connection you want for yourself now. Think about what you need to do to achieve each goal, and break them down into smaller steps if needed.

ENVISIONING A FUTURE CONNECTED YOU

Think about what it will feel like to have met your connection goals. What emotions or sensations do you hope to feel? Write a message to your future self, who has met these goals, specifically about how proud you feel of yourself for making such progress.

TURNING OUTWARD

Think about some people in your life to whom you would like to feel more connected. Reflect on what you appreciate about each of those people that makes you want to connect more deeply. How might you go about strengthening these connections?

REGULATE AS YOU RELATE

It's normal to have anxious thoughts or feelings when you push the edges of your comfort zone. When such emotions come up as you work toward your connection goals, turn inward and focus on your breathing. Take a deep breath in, hold it for a second, then release it fully, imagining that you are exhaling your negative feelings. Pause for a moment and reflect on the sense of calm settling in your body. Repeat this as many times as you need to.

CALLING UP YOUR INTERNAL RESERVES

Reflect on a time in the recent past when you felt motivated and confident. What was going on at the time? Where were you? What sensations can you recall? Write about what made you feel confident in those moments and what the sense of self-assuredness felt like in your body. Include any other thoughts you remember having during those moments.

NAMING THE HURDLES

What barriers do you see standing in the way of reaching your connection goals? Identify some obstacles that feel external to you, such as other people's communication skills or commitment level, or whether or not others will reciprocate your efforts. Then identify obstacles that are within you, such as your resistance to put yourself in novel situations or your fear that someone won't like you. For each internal obstacle, write about one thing you can do to try to lower or overcome that barrier.

"The most beautiful people we have known are those who have known defeat, known suffering, known struggle, known loss, and have found their way out of the depths. These persons have an appreciation, a sensitivity, and an understanding of life that fills them with compassion, gentleness, and a deep loving concern. Beautiful people do not just happen."

—Elisabeth Kübler-Ross
Death: The Final Stage of Growth

THE CONFIDENCE FACTOR

Explore the relationship between how confident you currently feel and your ultimate goals to achieve connection. How does confidence play into successfully reaching your goals? What are the ways you have learned to bring confidence to mind when you need it? How might this skill be helpful in going out and making new connections?

FIND YOUR POWER POSE

Think about what confidence feels like to you, and imagine a physical pose that embodies that feeling. It might be standing strong and tall like a mountain, adopting the stance of a powerful animal, or posing as if in the middle of some action. Try out different postures and see which one makes you feel most confident. This is your power pose! Draw a picture of it to remind yourself of this way of feeling and expressing your confidence.

My confidence gives me openness:
to new things, to new people, to new possibilities.

DOUBT REMOVAL

Reflect on any doubts you may hold about yourself that get in the way of connecting and exploring relationships with others. Write out as many doubts as you can identify. Then see how you can turn each doubtful statement into an affirming one. You might find a positive spin on a trait you've previously seen as negative. "I'm awkward" may turn into "It's okay that I'm awkward. It actually makes me funny and interesting."

RELATIONSHIP REWARDS

What were the feelings, events, interactions, or aspects of past relationships that were most rewarding to you? What did you like best about these relationships? Brainstorm as many fulfilling elements of these relationships as you can, then divide the list into actions by those people (e.g., "They did something kind for me") and ways they made you feel (e.g., "I felt loved when they . . ."). Reflect on the fact that satisfaction with relationships has to do with others' feelings and actions but also quite a bit with you and yours!

REACH OUT

Write a letter to a friend or loved one whom you haven't spoken to recently. Practice setting aside any worries about the closeness of the relationship or their potential response to receiving the letter. Focus instead on what would feel good to say to that person. Express what feels authentic to you and your relationship with them, and what you want them to know. Send your note to the recipient and congratulate yourself for reaching out.

CONFLICTED ABOUT CONFLICT

Sometimes we hold on to negative feelings about relationships because of conflict that occurred in them. Reflect on your feelings, thoughts, and beliefs about conflict in relationships. Next, read what you have written through a compassionate lens, noting any judgments or distorted beliefs you might be holding about yourself or others. Determine if an affirmation or a different perspective might be helpful in your thinking about conflict.

CONFLICT HAPPENS

Experiencing conflict is perfectly normal in relationships, but that doesn't mean we always handle conflict in ways that are healthy for us. John and Julie Gottman, married researchers, clinical psychologists, and founders of the Gottman Institute, say that the healthiest goal of conflict is mutual understanding. No matter what the disagreement is about, both people should recognize that each party has something important to convey. Reflect on how seeing understanding as the goal might change how you approach conflict in your relationships.

FROM SELF-LOVE TO OTHER-LOVE

Try seeing yourself through a more compassionate, self-empowered view. Does it make you feel stronger? More daring? Do you feel more able to empathize with others, having given attention to your own emotions? Write about how seeing yourself in a positive, self-loving light is likely to affect what you want out of relationships or how you might show up in them.

"Your self-love is a medicine for the earth."

—Yung Pueblo
Inward

CONSIDERING YOURSELF IN RELATIONSHIPS

Reflect on the strengths and uniqueness that you have brought to light about yourself and how these parts of you might shine in a relationship with another person. Also, consider your weaknesses or challenges, and with a compassionate view of them, reflect on how you might support and nurture yourself while in a relationship with someone else. How would you like to show up in your next relationship in a way that makes you feel good about yourself?

MAKE EYE CONTACT

Challenge yourself to make eye contact with the next person you see. Practice with yourself in the mirror first, looking yourself in the eyes and holding your gaze for a moment. Say an affirmation to yourself if it helps you feel brave and confident. When you next go out into the world, carry that courageous energy with you and look someone else in the eyes. Add a smile if you're feeling bold. Be sure to congratulate yourself afterward on a job well done.

REINTERPRETING DOUBTS

When you embarked on your eye-contact challenge, did you have any worries or negative thoughts before, during, or after the exercise? Write them down here and allow yourself to see those thoughts in a different way, using your self-reflection and compassion skills. Remind yourself that your own interpretation of things sometimes gets in your way, and ask whether you can try out another interpretation that makes you feel more confident and courageous.

I am capable of having fulfilling, satisfying relationships.

SELF SAFETY NET

Think about how you build trust with other people. What do you look for that allows you to trust someone? Are there things they can say or do that help you feel trusting? Write these things down and then revise those proof points for yourself: How can you build trust in yourself? What will allow you to trust yourself as you open yourself up to new experiences and connections? We need to be able to trust that we can care for whatever feelings may come up. How can you encourage this feeling of trusting yourself to be your own safety net?

THE BIG THREE

Researchers have identified three different types of loneliness we can feel: intimate loneliness, where we want a close, deep emotional connection that involves affection and trust; social loneliness, in which we want to connect with others who share interests and support; and collective loneliness, where we might be seeking a community with a shared purpose or broader connectivity. In the space below, write about how you experience loneliness in each of these categories—what you are seeking, how you have felt connected in this area in the past, and where/how you might work on your feelings of loneliness in each area.

Intimate Loneliness	Social Loneliness	Collective Loneliness

COMMUNITY CONNECTIONS

Identify some communities that you are a part of—this could be groups built around your interests, work-related groups, online communities, or people in your area. Reflect on communities that you would like to be a part of across any of those categories. Write down as many existing and aspirational communities for yourself as you can think of.

GROUP UP

Choose one of the communities you identified on page 149 that you would like to be a part of but aren't yet involved with. Research how you could join the group, or be in touch with any of its members, and do what you can to get involved. If you have to apply, fill out an application. If you need to connect personally with someone about your interest, find an address and write to them. Take the first steps to getting connected with a new community that might be fulfilling to you or expand your interests and network.

REFLECTION ON JOINING

Reflect on the work you've done or are currently doing toward joining a new community or group. What feelings came up for you along the way? Did you experience excitement? Fear? Did you have any negative thoughts about yourself or others as you were trying something new? Identify three key feelings you've experienced, as well as any thoughts you had about yourself or others, and write them down here. Look over what you've written and see whether there are any changes to your thinking that might make branching out more rewarding.

THE INTROVERT/ EXTROVERT DIMENSION

Part of our personalities is how we handle social interactions. Extroverts gain energy by being around other people, while introverts feel their energy drained by interaction and need alone time to replenish. Some people might feel a mix of both and be somewhere in the middle of the introvert-extrovert spectrum. Neither way of being is better than the other; they are just parts of us and our uniqueness. Identify where you fall on the introvert-extrovert spectrum. List out the pros and cons of being where you are on this continuum.

TAPPING INTO OUR SHARED HUMANITY

We are all unique, and yet we are all connected to each other through our shared humanity. We have similar experiences, thoughts, and feelings across time, distance, and cultures. Reflect on some of your challenges with the knowledge that many others have experienced similar struggles. Write about this concept of shared humanity, what it means to you, and how it can be helpful when you might be feeling lonely or isolated.

We are all connected. I am not alone.

WHAT SHARING SHOWS US

Think about a time when you shared an experience with someone else, either by doing something together or by talking about something that you'd both been through. Write about this shared experience and what was rewarding about having something in common with another person. Finally, reflect on how you felt about yourself in this interaction and what you learned about yourself through sharing.

WIDENING YOUR FRIEND ZONE

Think about how you might expand your friend group in small but meaningful ways. Who are the people in your life who are supportive of you and will help you nurture your dreams and goals? How can you spend more time with them? Be creative in thinking about how you can form and nurture friendships despite distance, or how you can engage with an acquaintance in the hopes of becoming better friends down the road.

TAKE THE FIRST STEP TO CONNECT

Take a step toward widening your social network or friend group. Reflect on someone you can reconnect with or become closer to and make the first move. You might write them a note, call them, or ask to get together. Acknowledge and allow any feelings that come up, and nurture yourself through them, but don't let them stop you from taking the first step toward connection.

THE WAITING GAME

What if you want to be closer to someone but they don't reciprocate your feelings? Or what if you reach out and you're left waiting for a response? When we can't control the outcome of an effort we've made, we have to practice acceptance. It will be okay either way. You will be okay. Reflect on some of the feelings you might have while waiting for a response, and write some compassionate and accepting words to yourself.

"The happiest of all lives
is a busy solitude."

–Voltaire

FRIENDSHIP REFLECTIONS

Consider your past friendships. What kinds of people are you usually drawn to for friendship? How have you typically gone about making friends? What emotions have you experienced in friendships? What efforts or gifts have you been willing to give to your friendships in the past? What have you received? Look over your reflections to see whether there are patterns, challenges, or a sense of balance in giving and receiving in your past friendships. What do you notice or want to change?

INTIMACY REFLECTIONS

Reflect on how you think about intimacy in your relationships, whether romantic or friendly. How do you feel emotionally close to someone? What helps you open up emotionally? Are there factors in the other person that can encourage feelings of intimacy for you? Do you have any fears or negative thoughts about intimacy? Write down your reflections. If you notice any unhelpful thoughts or beliefs, write about some ways you might counter or challenge them.

CONNECT THROUGH CREATIVITY

Take some quiet time to reflect on your hopes, dreams, and emotions about relationships and connections with others. Then, using whatever creative medium you have accessible or feel most comfortable with, create a visual expression of your feelings. You can make a collage, a painting, a drawing, abstract art, or an audio track that captures your emotions. When you have finished, take in your creation with wonder and appreciation. Think about ways you might share your art with others, either by virtually posting it somewhere or by individually sending someone a picture of it. Creative expression connects us with our own emotions and can also connect us with others.

STRENGTHS AND LIMITATIONS AS CONNECTIVE MATERIAL

Reflect on the personal strengths and limitations you have identified about yourself throughout the course of this journal. Write down three strengths that you possess and three limitations that you struggle with. Consider that these characteristics, whether you see them as positive or negative, are the very things that connect you with other people. Write about ways you could connect with others through the strengths and limitations you have identified.

PROJECTING COMPASSION OUTWARD

Recall how you have practiced self-compassion by being mindful of what emotions you were feeling, taking a kind, gentle approach to yourself and letting go of judgments that inspire unhelpful ideas about what you should or shouldn't feel. Consider how you can extend this same approach to others. How can you recognize where judgments of others are getting in your way of relating with or being compassionate toward them?

PRACTICE LOVING KINDNESS

Take a few moments to practice a loving-kindness meditation when you feel lonely or might be seeking a sense of calm, caring, and connectedness. First, think about yourself and think or say these words out loud, allowing them to sink in deeply.

May I be happy.

May I be healthy and strong.

May I be filled with loving kindness.

May I be peaceful and free.

Repeat the exercise, this time aiming the words at a loved one, then at someone you have trouble getting along with, and finally at all people everywhere.

Adapted from Sharon Salzberg's guided loving-kindness meditation at Mindful.org.

BASKING IN YOUR CONNECTED GLOW

Reflect on how you are at your very best when you feel connected, internally and externally. Describe yourself in this lovely, connected state. What are you like? How do you feel? As you write each descriptor, allow yourself to feel this way now, and enjoy the feelings of connectedness that you actually hold within you all the time.

I am worthy and capable of deep connection.

FOCUSING ON THE FUTURE

Look back at your connection goals on page 3 and write down what steps you have already taken to achieve them. You might choose to revise your goals now that you have a deeper understanding of what connection means to you and how you feel most connected. Reflect on what you have already done to approach your goals and give yourself congratulations on the brave steps you have taken. For each goal, identify the next steps. How will you know when you achieve your goal? And what will you do to celebrate when you do?

COMMENCE: THE ENDING IS JUST THE BEGINNING

Take those bigger steps toward your connection goals. If you have been putting off an action that will help you feel more connected in the ways you want to, make a plan for that big move. Give yourself the validation and compassion you need to acknowledge that you are taking on a significant challenge. Allow yourself to feel any fears and push yourself to do it anyway. Plan for obstacles and adjust as needed. Celebrate yourself for taking the leap. The outcome is less important than the courage it takes to go outside of your comfort zone.

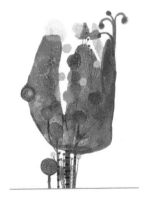

REFERENCES

Babauta, Leo. "A Simple Method to Avoid Being Judgmental (yes, that means you!)." ZenHabits.net. Accessed November 10, 2020. ZenHabits.net/a-simple-method-to-avoid-being-judgmental-yes-that-means-you.

Brach, Tara. "Resources ~ RAIN: Recognize, Allow, Investigate, Nurture." TaraBrach.com. Accessed November 2, 2020. TaraBrach.com/rain.

Brown, Brené. *I Thought It Was Just Me (But It Isn't): Making the Journey from "What Will People Think" to "I Am Enough."* New York: Avery, 2007.

Brown, Joshua, and Joel Wong. *"How Gratitude Changes You and Your Brain." Greater Good Magazine.* June 6, 2017. GreaterGood.Berkeley.edu/article/item/how_gratitude_changes_you_and_your_brain.

Chapman, Gary. *The Five Love Languages: How to Express Heartfelt Commitment to Your Mate.* Chicago: Northfield Publishing, 1992.

De Souza, Vacir. *Group Psychotherapy: Exercises at Hand, Volume 1.* Bloomington, IN: iUniverse, 2011.

Emmons, Henry. *The Chemistry of Joy: A Three-Step Program for Overcoming Depression Through Western Science and Eastern Wisdom.* New York: Fireside, 2006.

The Foundation for Art and Healing. "The UnLonely Project." Accessed December 10, 2020. ArtAndHealing.org/unlonely-home.

Gottman, John, and Julie Schwartz Gottman. *Eight Dates: Essential Conversations for a Lifetime of Love.* New York: Workman Publishing, 2018.

Grohol, John M. "15 Common Cognitive Distortions." Psych Central. May 17, 2016. PsychCentral.com/lib/15-common-cognitive-distortions.

Kuchinskas, Susan. *The Chemistry of Connection: How the Oxytocin Response Can Help You Find Trust, Intimacy, and Love.* Oakland, CA: New Harbinger Publications, Inc., 2009.

Masi, Christopher M., Hsi-Yuan Chen, Louise C. Hawkley, and John T. Cacioppo. "A Meta-Analysis of Interventions to Reduce Loneliness." *Personality and Social Psychology Review* 15, no. 3 (2011): 222. doi:10.1177/1088868310377394.

Mind Tools. "SMART Goals: How to Make Your Goals Achievable." *Mind Tools.* Accessed November 12, 2020. MindTools.com/pages/article/smart-goals.htm.

MindWise. "Lifestyle Changes to Manage Your Mood." *Mindwise Innovations*. Accessed November 27, 2020. https://www.mindwise.org/blog/community/lifestyle-changes-to-manage-your-mood/.

Murthy, Vivek H. *Together: The Healing Power of Human Connection in a Sometimes Lonely World.* New York: HarperCollins, 2020.

Neff, Kristin. "Self-Compassion: An Alternative Conceptualization of a Healthy Attitude Toward Oneself." *Self and Identity* 2, no. 2 (2003): 85. doi:10.1080/15298860309032.

Oettingen, Gabriele. *Rethinking Positive Thinking: Inside the New Science of Motivation.* New York: Penguin Random House, 2014.

Pennock, Seph F., and Hugo Alberts. "Positive Psychology Toolkit." PositivePsychology.com. Accessed November 4, 2020. PositivePsychology.com/toolkit/.

Peters, Madelon L., Ida K. Flink, Katja Boersma, and Steven J. Linton. "Manipulating Optimism: Can Imagining a Best Possible Self Be Used to Increase Positive Future Expectancies?" *The Journal of Positive Psychology* 5, no. 3 (2010): 204–211. doi:10.1080/17439761003790963.

Salzberg, Sharon. "A Guided Loving-Kindness Meditation with Sharon Salzberg." *Mindful* (blog). The Foundation for a Mindful Society. May 14, 2020. https://www.mindful.org/a-guided-loving-kindness-meditation-with-sharon-salzberg/.

Schauer, Maggie, Frank Neuner, Katy Robjant, and Thomas Elbert. *Narrative Exposure Therapy.* Cambridge, MA: Hogrefe & Huber Publishers, 2005.

Schwartz, Richard. "Evolution of the Internal Family Systems Model." IFS Institute. Accessed November 14, 2020. https://ifs-institute.com/resources/articles/evolution-internal-family-systems-model-dr-richard-schwartz-ph-d.

Sciangula, Antonella, and Marian M. Morry. "Self-Esteem and Perceived Regard: How I See Myself Affects My Relationship Satisfaction." *The Journal of Social Psychology* 149, no. 2 (2009): 154. doi:10.3200/SOCP.149.2.143-158.

Scott, Elizabeth. "Effects of Conflict and Stress on Relationships." *Verywell Mind.* July 24, 2020. VerywellMind.com/the-toll-of-conflict-in-relationships-3144952.

Seligman, Martin E. P. *Authentic Happiness: Using the New Positive Psychology to Realize Your Potential for Lasting Fulfillment.* New York: Free Press, 2002.

Seligman, Martin E. P. *Learned Optimism: How to Change Your Mind and Your Life.* New York: Free Press, 2006.

US Institute for Environmental Conflict Resolution. "Non-Judgmental Language: Helpful Phrases." Training Workshop on Introduction to Managing Environmental Conflict, Washington, D.C., September 14–15, 2010. Accessed November 10, 2020. UWSP.edu/hr/Documents/Site%20Documents/Human%20Resources/Non-Judgemental%20Language%20for%20Feedback.pdf.

White, Donna M. "Challenging Our Cognitive Distortions and Creating Positive Outlooks." Psych Central. May 17, 2016. https://psychcentral.com/lib/challenging-our-cognitive-distortions-and-creating-positive-outlooks#1.

ABOUT THE AUTHOR

Jessie Everts, PhD, LMFT, is a therapist, mom, yoga/mindfulness teacher, author, and mental health consultant. She uses mindfulness practices along with cognitive and acceptance therapies to work with individuals who might be struggling with anxiety, life transitions, parenting, postpartum mental health, work-life balance, and trauma. Dr. Everts received her doctorate in family social science from the University of Minnesota and is a licensed marriage and family therapist. She is passionate about bringing mental health knowledge and skills to people outside of the therapy office, and helping people feel more self-compassionate and connected. She lives in Minnesota with her spouse and two strong-willed children.